PENNSYLVANIA

A PHOTOGRAPHIC CELEBRATION

photography by
Terry Wild
unless otherwise indicated

compiled by the staff of
American Geographic Publishing

Above: Old and new in Philadelphia.
Right: Autumn farmscape, Lycoming County
Facing page: Near Spartansburg, Warren County.

Front cover: Aerial view of Lycoming County.
Title page: Bastress Township farm, Lycoming County.
Back cover, top: View of the fleet docks, Pittsburgh.
Bottom left: November countryside
Right: Out for a ride

ISBN 0-938314-71-8

© 1989 American Geographic Publishing
P.O. Box 5630, Helena, MT 59604. (406) 443-2842
Photography © 1989 Terry Wild unless otherwise credited

William A. Cordingley, Chairman
Rick Graetz, Publisher & CEO
Mark O. Thompson, Director of Publications
Barbara Fifer, Production Manager

Design by Linda Collins.
Printed in Hong Kong by DNP America, Inc., San Francisco

American Geographic Publishing is a corporation for publishing illustrated geographic information and guides. It is not associated with American Geographical Society. It has no commercial or legal relationship to and should not be confused with any other company, society or group using the words geographic or geographical in its name or its publications.

Terry Wild, whose studio is a converted barn in the Nippenose Valley near Williamsport, graduated from Lycoming College, Williamsport and The Art Center College of Design, Los Angeles. He specializes in commercial, industrial and editorial photography. His work has been exhibited in one-man and group shows around Pennsylvania and the nation, and has appeared in numerous national publications.

Above: *From the Gateway Clipper, fleet docks at Pittsburgh.*
Facing page: *Fort Pitt Bridge over the Monongahela River, and downtown Pittsburgh.*

Above: Constitution Bridge over the Susquehanna at Lock Haven.
Left: The Enola trainyard.

Above: *Towanda Creek, Bradford County.*
Right: *Amish farmers baling hay near Elimsport.*
Facing page: *LTV Steel Works, the sole steel plant operating in Pittsburgh.*

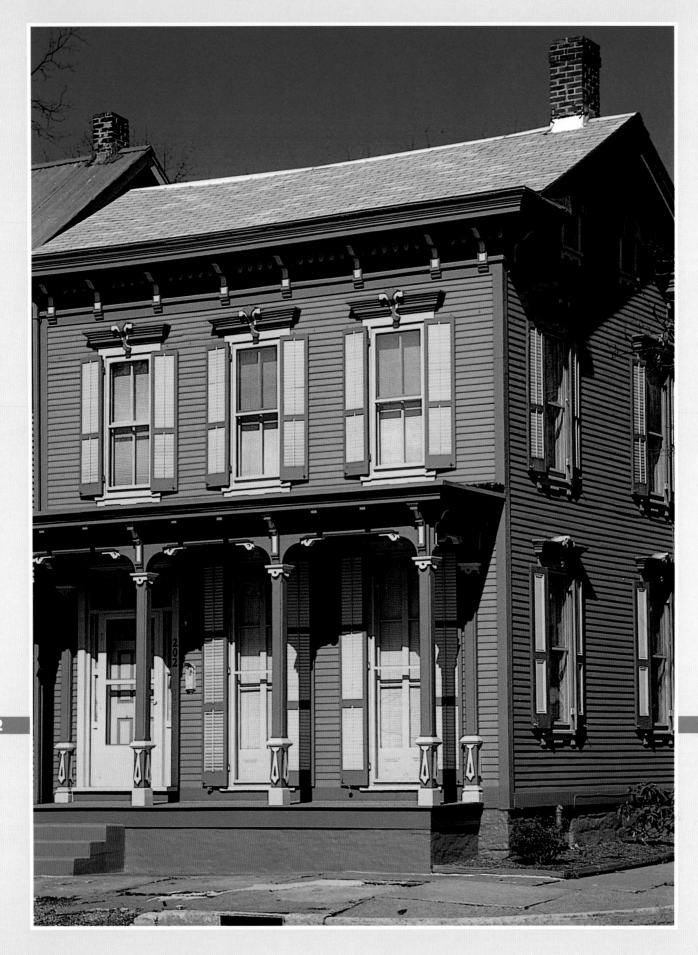

Above: *State Capitol, Harrisburg.*
Right: *Chanticleer.*
Facing page: *Victorian style in Lewisburg.*

13

15

Above: Sunrise over Bradford County.
Facing page: At the Bedford Festival of Apple Growers.

Above: "Song to Nature," by Victor David Brenner, University of Pittsburgh.
Facing page: Lock Haven and the West Branch of the Susquehanna.

Above: Coal barges on the Monongahela at Pittsburgh.
Right: Cook Forest State Park, Forest County.
Facing page: Calliope at the West Branch Promenade, Williamsport.

21

Above: *Trax Hall Cupola, Bucknell University, Lewisburg.*
Left: *The Nippenose Valley, Lycoming County.*

Above: *Philadelphia's Christmas Parade.*
Right: *Retired farmers Eleanor and John Miller, Centre Hall, Huntingdon County.*
Facing page: *Canoeing the Susquehanna in Lycoming County.*

Above: Montour County farmscape.
Right: Ein Prosit zur Gemütlichkeit!
Yuengling Brewery Tap Room,
Pottsville.
Facing page: White-tailed deer fawn.
Kelly Cooper photo.

Above: Franklin and Marshall College, Lancaster.
Left: Behemoths at the Lamar Truck Stop, Clinton County.
Facing page: Autumn symphony, Lycoming County.

Above: Wilkes Barre.
Left: Rose Valley Lake, Lycoming County.

29

Above: *The old gymnasium at Lafayette College, Easton.*
Facing page: *On the Susquehanna River in Northumberland County.*

Above: The Hiawatha paddleboat on the Susquehanna at Williamsport.
Left: Marywood College rotunda, Scranton.
Facing page: Winter symmetry in Cook Forest State Park.

Above: An abundance of cabbages.
Right: The dignified Market Street, Selinsgrove.

Above and left: At Williamsport Bills baseball games.

Above: *At the ready: Danville fireman Mark Anderman*
Right: *Hillsgrove church, Lycoming County.*
Facing page: *Presque Isle and Lake Erie.*

Above: At Allegheny College, Meadville.
Right: Autumn in peaceful Collomsville.

Above: *Ready for winter.*
Facing page: *Maple trees and the first hint of autumn.*

Above: *A delicate layer of ice decorates delicate moss.*
Right: *When the frost is on the pumpkin in Lycoming County.*

Above: The gliding Judsons.
Facing page: Lilypond on a cloudy day in Lycoming County.

Above: Eastern wild turkey jakes.
Kelly Cooper photo.
Left: Maple sugaring time,
Lycoming County.
Facing page: Putting in on the
Susquehanna, Clearfield County.

Above: *Crawford County barn cat.*
Left: *Rock Run in the Tiadaghton State Forest.*

Above: Fisheye view of the Tiadaghton State Forest.
Left: In Black Moshannon State Park, Centre County.

Above: *Row houses in Reading.*
Left: *Athens-area dairy farmer Anthony Barrett.*
Facing page: *In Columbia County.*

Above: *Ice filigree.*
Right: *Near two pots of gold in Lycoming County. M. Anderman photo.*

Above: Hillsgrove lumber mill.
Left: A warning well taken on Route 880 near Loganton.
Facing page: Time exposure of Rock Run terraces, Tiadaghton State Forest.

Above: *A restored stone barn along Route 87 near Montoursville.*
Left: *Misty woods, Lycoming County.*

Above: *The secrets of bobbin lace making revealed at the West Branch Promenade, Williamsport.*
Facing page: *High Victorian style in Lewisburg.*

Above: Pop Warner football at Jersey Shore.
Facing page: In Lewisburg.

Lycoming County corn crib and farmscape.

Above: *University of Pennsylvania, Philadelphia.*
Left: *Tioga City.*

Above: *Denizen of Williamsport.*
Right: *Winter chores, Lewisburg.*
Facing page: *Coal-fired power plant, Washingtonville, Montour County.*

Above: *Montour County quarter horses.*
Right: *Ricketts Glen State Park.*

Above: Don Daughenbaugh fishing Loyalsock Creek, Lycoming County.
Facing page: Harvest time near Freeburg, Snyder County.

Above: Scranton.
Right: At Allenwood.
Facing page, top: Near Mifflin-burg.
Bottom: Spring plowing in the Nippenose Valley.

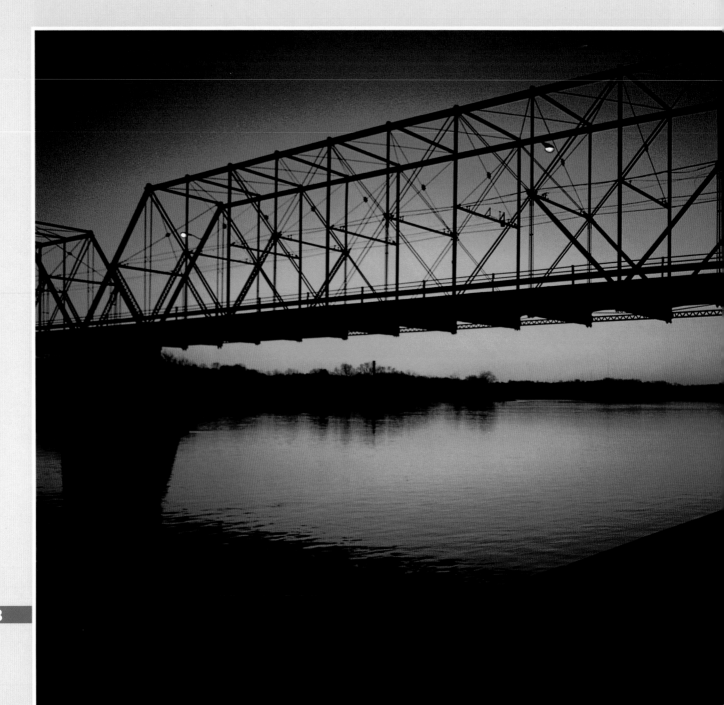

Above: *University of Pennsylvania sculling team on the Schuylkill River at Philadelphia.*
Left: *Walking bridge at Harrisburg.*

Above: *Weis Center for Performing Arts at Bucknell University.*
Facing page: *Pennsylvania State Capitol.*

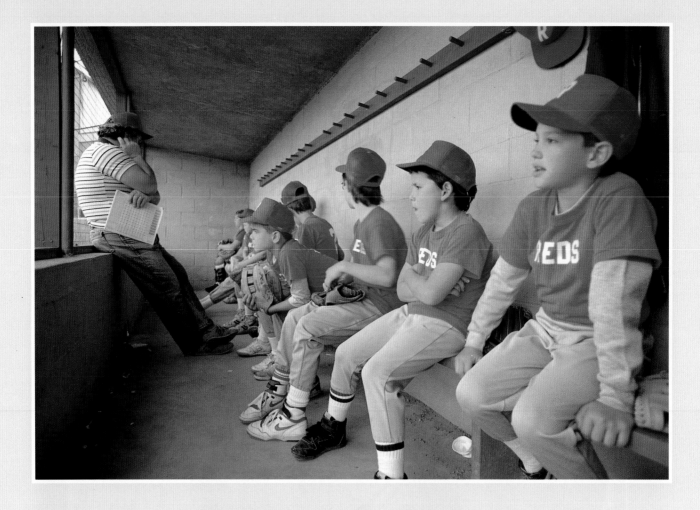

Above and left: A tense team and the crowd at the Little League World Series, Williamsport.
Facing page: Newsgirls in costume for the West Branch Promenade, Williamsport.

Above: Ruffed grouse, Pennsylvania's state bird. Conrad Rowe photo.
Right: Combining wheat near Elimsport
Facing page: Joe Palooka in Wilkes Barre.

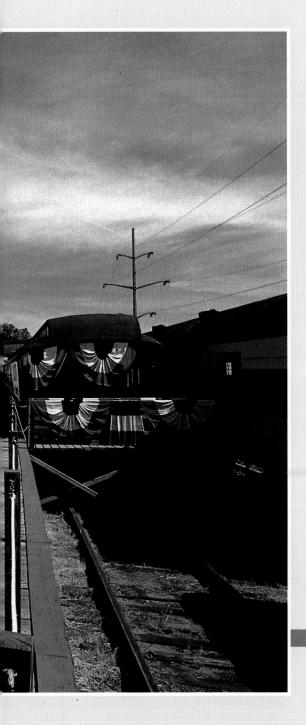

Top: Angora goats, Lycoming County.
Above: The Tom Quick Inn, Milford.
Left: The Hilton/Lackawanna Building and Train Museum, Scranton.

Above: Railroad bridge at Harrisburg.
Left: Football season at Bucknell University.
Facing page: Oil refinery, Chester County.

Above: Black bears still roam mountain forests.
Conrad Rowe photo.
Right: Late-summer lushness in Tioga County.
Facing page: World's End State Park.

Above: Adventures at the Philadelphia Zoo.
Right: Bicycling Lycoming County.

Above: *Route 220 crossing Pine Creek, Clinton County.*
Right: *Immaculate Conception Church, Bastress Township, Lycoming County.*
Facing page: *The Nescopec River in Luzerne County.*
Overleaf: *Kitchen's Creek Falls in Ricketts Glen State Park.*